CH

THE STATES AND THEIR SYMBOLS

New Hampshire
Facts and Symbols

by Muriel L. Dubois

Consultant:
William Copeley, Librarian
New Hampshire Historical Society

Hilltop Books
an imprint of Capstone Press
Mankato, Minnesota

Hilltop Books are published by Capstone Press
151 Good Counsel Drive, P.O. Box 669, Mankato, Minnesota 56002
http://www.capstone-press.com

Library of Congress Cataloging-in-Publication Data
Dubois, Muriel L.
    New Hampshire facts and symbols / by Muriel L. Dubois.
        p. cm.—(The states and their symbols)
    Includes bibliographical references and index.
    Summary: Presents information about the state of New Hampshire, its
nickname, motto, and emblems.
        ISBN 0-7368-0524-9
        1. Emblems, State—New Hampshire—Juvenile literature. [1. Emblems, State—
New Hampshire. 2. New Hampshire.] I. Title. II. Series.
CR203.N67 D84 2000
974.2—dc21
                                                                    99-053461
                                                                         CIP

Editorial Credits
Tom Adamson, editor; Linda Clavel, production designer and illustrator;
  Kimberly Danger, photo researcher

Photo Credits
David Liebman, 16
International Stock/Andre Jenny, 10
Jeff March, 14
New Hampshire Historical Society #S1999.502.73, 6
One Mile Up, Inc., 8, 10 (inset)
Photri-Microstock, 22 (bottom)
Rob and Ann Simpson, cover
Robert McCaw, 12
Root Resources/Alan G. Nelson, 18; A. B. Sheldon, 20
Unicorn Stock Photos/Andre Jenny, 22 (top)
Visuals Unlimited/Dick Poe, 22 (middle)

1 2 3 4 5 6 05 04 03 02 01 00

Table of Contents

Canada

NEW HAMPSHIRE

Maine

Vermont

Connecticut River

🏛 Franconia Notch
State Park

Lake
Winnipesaukee

Merrimack River

Atlantic
Ocean

Christa McAuliffe
Planetarium 🏛

Concord ⭐

🏛 Strawbery Banke
Museum

Manchester ⚪

Massachusetts

⭐ Capital

⚪ City

🏛 Places to
Visit

〰 River

Fast Facts

Capital: Concord is the capital of New Hampshire.

Largest City: Manchester is the largest city in New Hampshire. More than 103,000 people live there.

Size: New Hampshire covers 9,304 square miles (24,097 square kilometers). It is the 46th largest state.

Location: New Hampshire is in the northeastern United States.

Population: 1,185,048 people live in New Hampshire (U.S. Census Bureau, 1998 estimate).

Statehood: On June 21, 1788, New Hampshire became the ninth state to join the United States.

Natural Resources: Lumber is New Hampshire's most important natural resource. New Hampshire's lakes and rivers are important to its tourism industry.

Manufactured Goods: New Hampshire factory workers make electrical equipment, machinery, and paper products.

Crops: New Hampshire farmers grow apple trees and pine trees. Strawberries, blueberries, hay, sweet corn, and maple syrup also are important products.

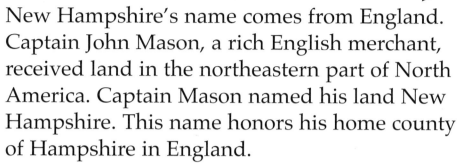

New Hampshire's name comes from England. Captain John Mason, a rich English merchant, received land in the northeastern part of North America. Captain Mason named his land New Hampshire. This name honors his home county of Hampshire in England.

New Hampshire is called the Granite State. Granite is a hard stone used in buildings. Workers dig granite from huge pits called quarries. Granite is strong and lasts a long time. The nickname Granite State shows that people from New Hampshire are strong like granite.

Workers used New Hampshire granite to make many famous buildings. The Jefferson Memorial and the Library of Congress in Washington, D.C., are made of New Hampshire granite. The United Nations building in New York City also is made of New Hampshire granite.

Workers dig granite from quarries. In the past, granite quarrying was an important business in New Hampshire.

State Seal and Motto

New Hampshire's government adopted its state seal in 1931. The seal represents the state's government. It also makes government papers official.

A picture of a frigate appears in the center of the seal. This warship is called the *Raleigh*. New Hampshire was an important shipbuilding center during the Revolutionary War (1775–1783). Laurel wreaths surround the ship. They are a symbol of victory. Behind the *Raleigh*, the sun rises above the ocean.

New Hampshire's motto, "Live Free or Die," appears on its license plates. General John Stark said, "Live free or die; death is not the worst of evils." General Stark was a Revolutionary War hero. He fought for America's freedom from England. He wanted to remind people that freedom is important. State officials approved the motto in 1945.

The granite boulder in the seal's foreground shows that New Hampshire is the Granite State.

State Capitol and Flag

Concord is the capital of New Hampshire. New Hampshire's capitol building is in Concord. Government officials meet there to make New Hampshire's laws.

Workers finished building New Hampshire's capitol in 1819. The capitol housed the state library and Supreme Court until 1895. Today, the governor and government officials meet in the capitol.

The capitol's dome is copper. Workers painted the dome with gold. A copper eagle stands at the top of the dome. The eagle's head is turned to the right to represent peace.

State officials adopted New Hampshire's flag in 1909. The flag has a dark blue background. The state seal appears in the center. Gold laurel leaves and nine gold stars surround the state seal. The stars show that New Hampshire was the ninth state to join the United States.

Workers built the capitol with granite from a Concord quarry.

State Bird

The purple finch became New Hampshire's state bird in 1957. The male finch has a dark red head. This color sometimes looks so dark it appears purple. The male's back is red-brown. The female finch is dull brown. Purple finches are about 6 inches (15 centimeters) long.

Purple finches have cone-shaped bills. Their bills help them eat seeds and insects. The birds also eat sunflower seeds from bird feeders. During summer, they eat fruit.

A male and a female purple finch build the nest together. They line the cup-shaped nest with twigs and feathers. The female purple finch lays about four blue-green eggs in spring.

Both parents care for the young birds. The parents build another nest after the young birds fly away. They raise a second family before the end of summer.

The purple finch eats many insects that harm crops.

State Tree

In 1947, New Hampshire adopted the white birch as its state tree. The white birch is tall and narrow. The tree can grow to be about 80 feet (24 meters) tall. The bark is white with black marks. It can be peeled off the tree. Birch bark feels like paper. Early settlers sometimes wrote on birch bark.

Native Americans used birch wood and bark to make many everyday items. They crafted baskets, baby carriers, and snowshoes. They also made spears, bows, and arrows from birch wood.

Native Americans also used birch bark to make lightweight canoes. New Hampshire's rivers sometimes became too shallow or rocky. The canoes were light enough to carry over land when the rivers were not passable.

Some animals, such as moose and deer, eat birch bark in winter. Hares, porcupines, and beavers also eat the bark.

White birch trees grow throughout New Hampshire.

State Flower

State officials named the purple lilac New Hampshire's state flower in 1919. New Hampshire's early settlers brought the purple lilac from England. Governor Benning Wentworth had lilac bushes planted outside his house in 1750.

The purple lilac blooms in May. The flowers grow in large, colorful clusters. The flowers have a sweet smell.

Lilac bushes can grow about 15 feet (4.6 meters) tall. They grow well in different kinds of soil. Purple lilac bushes live for a long time. People often plant lilacs around their homes for decoration.

The purple lilac produces many dark green leaves. Many types of birds like to nest in this thick green cover.

People in New Hampshire often plant the purple lilac in gardens.

State Animal

In 1983, New Hampshire adopted the white-tailed deer as its state animal. The white-tailed deer is a medium-sized deer. Male deer can weigh up to 300 pounds (140 kilograms). Female deer can weigh up to 200 pounds (90 kilograms).

The white-tailed deer is red-brown in summer and gray-brown in winter. The deer has white fur on the bottom of its tail. A deer raises its tail when it is frightened. The white on its tail signals other deer of danger.

Male deer are called bucks. Antlers grow on their heads. The antlers fall off each spring. New antlers grow throughout the summer. Female deer are called does. They give birth to one, two, or three fawns. Fawns have spots for the first few months of their lives.

White-tailed deer eat green plants, acorns, and nuts in summer and fall. In winter, they eat twigs and tree bark.

The white-tailed deer also is called the Virginia deer.

More State Symbols

State Amphibian: The red-spotted newt became the state amphibian in 1985. Young newts are called red efts. They are orange with black and red spots. Adult newts are olive green.

State Butterfly: The Karner blue butterfly is an endangered species. Construction destroyed much of its natural habitat. The Karner blue lives only in a few places in the United States. State officials chose the Karner blue as the state butterfly in 1992.

State Insect: The ladybug, or ladybird beetle, became the state insect in 1977. Fifth-grade students in Concord suggested naming a state insect.

State Rock: In 1985, New Hampshire officials chose granite as the state rock. Granite quarrying was once an important New Hampshire industry.

State Wildflower: The pink lady slipper became the state wildflower in 1991. The lady slipper blooms in May. The flower grows in moist areas near pine trees.

The Karner blue butterfly's wingspan is about 1 inch (2.5 centimeters).

Places to Visit

Christa McAuliffe Planetarium

The Christa McAuliffe Planetarium is in Concord. Christa McAuliffe was the first teacher in the United States to become an astronaut. Visitors to the planetarium see models of planets and stars projected onto a curved ceiling. They also participate in rocket-building workshops.

Franconia Notch State Park

Franconia Notch State Park is in the White Mountains. The park is the home of "The Old Man of the Mountain." This rock formation looks like the side view of an old man's face. Visitors swim in Echo Lake or hike through Flume Gorge. They also take a tramway ride up Cannon Mountain.

Strawbery Banke Museum

Strawbery Banke Museum is a restored 1800s seaport neighborhood in Portsmouth. Visitors tour furnished homes, shop in an old-fashioned general store, and learn historic games. Visitors also watch potters, boat makers, and other craftspeople.

Words to Know

antlers (ANT-lurz)—bony structures that grow on a deer's head

canoe (kuh-NOO)—a narrow boat that people move through the water with paddles; Native Americans made lightweight canoes out of birch bark.

endangered species (en-DAYN-jurd SPEE-seez)—a type of plant or animal in danger of dying out completely

fawn (FAWN)—a young deer

frigate (FRIG-it)—a warship used in the 1700s and 1800s

merchant (MUR-chuhnt)—a person who buys or sells things for profit

quarry (KWOR-ee)—a place where stones are dug or cut from the ground

tramway (TRAM-way)—a carrier that travels on a cable; a tramway carries people to the top of a mountain.

Read More

Kummer, Patricia K. *New Hampshire*. One Nation. Mankato, Minn.: Capstone Books, 1998.

Otfinoski, Steven. *New Hampshire*. Celebrate the States. New York: Benchmark Books, 1999.

Thompson, Kathleen. *New Hampshire*. Portrait of America. Austin, Texas: Raintree Steck-Vaughn, 1996.

Useful Addresses

New Hampshire
  Secretary of State
107 North Main Street
Concord, NH 03301-4989

New Hampshire
  State Library
20 Park Street
Concord, NH 03301

Internet Sites

New Hampshire Almanac
http://www.state.nh.us/nhinfo
New Hampshire Visitor's Guide
http://www.nhweb.com/travel_guide
Welcome to New Hampshire
http://www.visitnh.gov/index.php3

Index